Gym for the Soul

Gym
for the
Soul

Poems for a Spiritual Workout

Jim Deeds

First published in 2018
in Great Britain by
New City

© 2018 Jim Deeds

Illustrations supplied by the author and by Pixabay

Graphic designer Sandor Bartus

British Cataloguing-in-Publication Data:
A catalogue record for this book is available from the
British Library

ISBN 978-1-905039-35-7

Typeset in Great Britain by
New City, London

Printed and bound by Books Factory

CONTENTS

Chapter 3: Relationships 51

Chapter 4: Facing Hardships 63

Chapter 5: Mountain Moments 79

Introduction

Gym for the Soul is a book of poetry inspired by the quest to find God in the everyday nuts and bolts of life's experiences. The title refers to workout, something we can do each day – a spiritual workout – if only we keep our eyes and ears open for God among us.

The book is set out in 6 chapters, each dealing with particular experiences we go through in life. From dealing with death and loss to experiencing moments of spiritual insight in nature; from going through hardships to celebrating the good times of new life and love, it encompasses the breadth and depth of the human condition.

This book will appeal to a variety of readers, and can, of course, be simply used as any other bundle of poetry. However, one might also treat it as a daily prayer companion, because each of the poems takes the reader deeper into the internal, spiritual world.

Given the nature of each chapter, this book might work out as a companion to the reader in coping with grief or loss of faith, helping in the search for meaning or simply revelling in the beauty of nature and the wonder of human relationships.

Gym for the Soul as a title comes from a comment made by a young man in a secondary school where I am regularly invited to speak to the students on matters of faith and spirituality. Hearing that I was coming in to speak to their class immediately after their P.E. exercises, he said: 'Jim's class is like going to the gym for our souls.' When I heard this remark, it stuck with me and inspired me to use it as the idea behind this book.

In the pages of *Gym for the Soul*, we are invited to do a workout and at the same time to work out the big questions of life – all in the presence of the God in all things.

Jim Deeds

Chapter 1: The Bigger Plan

'I know the plans I have for you, says the Lord.'
Jeremiah 29:11

In this chapter you will find poems which reflect the things we see around us that suggest that there is a bigger plan to life than our own little one. Our own plan is usually based on our (limited) experience of life and unless we are very careful, our own plan may be all about meeting our own needs. However, as we grow through life and try to look at the world around us we begin to see differently. We see things and situations that, though they don't seem to make sense – suffering, mistakes, failures – begin to fall into a pattern of a bigger plan at work; one in which we all have a part to play and one in which we all can learn through these very experiences. This chapter is an encouragement to all of us to see the whole picture of life; the divine imprint if you will; the bigger plan. Allow these poems to fall on your ears and your heart and ask yourself, 'where is the bigger plan at work in the world around me?'

The Sound that God Makes

There is a sound that God makes
One sound, heard in a multitude of ways
Bursting through to a world whose hearing has been dulled
Through years of the white noise of disconnection

God's sound, heard and felt
When hearing and feeling is who we are
We hear it in a new-born's scream of arrival
In the last breath drawn in awe at the journey just beginning

In the midst of the raucous cheers of joy and delight
God's sound is there, celebrating
And comforting those in grief
God's sound harmonises with their cries

Watch out for the moments of unexpected kindness
Of experiences of love and forgiveness not deserved
These moments are the vibrations resultant
Of God's sound at work through us, with us, in us

Catch yourself saying something so good
So pure in intent and other-orientated
That it doesn't sound like you anymore
But another, and know it is Another speaking

In silence, sit and listen
Connect to that part of you that you are coming to know
In that place you will hear a feint, gentle sound building within
Growing in intensity – 'yes', it says

Become Incarnate

Become incarnate in me
In words of unity and peace
Become incarnate in me
In actions of love and humility
Become incarnate in me
In giving up my rights for others
Become incarnate in me
In knowing your love and showering others with it
Become incarnate in the world
Through plenty, shared
Become incarnate in the world
Through peace treaties and surrender
Become incarnate in the world
Through deep understanding of our oneness
Become incarnate in the world
Through the hands and feet of all people
Become incarnate in the hungry
Let them be fed
Become incarnate in the homeless
Let them know shelter
Become incarnate in the outcast
Let them know community
Become incarnate in the vulnerable
Let them know protection
Become incarnate in the proud
In moments of falling
Become incarnate in the rich
In moments of giving
Become incarnate in the judgemental
In moments of unity with the judged

Become incarnate in the warmongers
In moments of knowing the suffering of the victims of war
Become incarnate
Born in temporary accommodation
Become incarnate
Born of a refugee family, fleeing
Become incarnate
Born into a world of persecution
Become incarnate
Born once and for all
Become incarnate
Today

The Intercessor

Her eyes open slowly
The familiar pattern of nightly waking
Into a darkness and silence
An empty space full of purpose

'Someone needs a prayer'
Compassion is calling this night
Who might it be this time?
She consents: 'Show me. I'll pray'

As she lies there at one
With her God and her mission
To pray for the needy
A name or a face soon appears

And with it she sighs
There is relief: 'Now I know'
But there is grief in the sigh
As she connects with their pain

Lying silently, she prays
For a soul who knows nothing
Of her nightly campaign
Of compassion for the world

In the morning's bright dawn
She lights a little candle
And puts another name in her book
So full it groans with the load

Her day proceeds slowly
Tired, but things to be done
One eye on the life she leads
The other on her prayed-for one

You Are I Am

The sunshine comes, illuminating all
With rays of purest gold-heat
Setting is inevitable, daily
And with night it goes again

But you are always

Leaves, once green, dry brown
(Wrinkled skin of the tree)
Break from their source
And fall to the ground

But always, you are

The tide floods the beach and fishes dart
Kaleidoscopic oceanic excitement results
But only for a while,
Tide receded and they are gone

Always, though, you are

Youth, with all its folly
And carefree nonsense
Lives but for a fleeting moment
And old age walks gingerly in its footprints

Not you – always, you are

Understanding, intellect and ability
Kick-start conversation and debate
We must grow into quietness
As these gifts pass

No passing for you, you are always

This body of ours
Sinew, cartilage and blood
Slowly decays until it is dust
And we go

Where you are.

Candle Wisdom

I held the candle
In my gaze, intently
Closely, until I felt
Its heat, heat me

The flame danced
Bright orange glow
Tempting me, inwards
To the centre

The space inside the flame
Blue, cool mystery
Co-existent with the glow
Refuge from the heat

And in the quiet, cool
Centre of all things
Enlightenment, lighter
Yes, it is good.

Sacred Dance of the Trinity

Sacred dance of love
Circular, as one body
Each holding the other
In gazes, adoring

Endless and timeless
The very nature of things
Comes forth
Threefold, singular in vision

Tripartite effusion
Chloroform of love
Heady, dizzy
Fill me, send me

Walking

Walking and praying,
Praying and walking,
Walking and talking,
Talking to God.

Living and praying,
Praying is living,
Living for this time,
Time to stand still.

Quietness and praying,
Praying in silence,
Words do not matter,
Presence is all.

Praying is listening,
Listening to all prayers,
God always hears us,
Will we all hear God?

Business and busyness,
Buzzing and action,
What are we acting,
If not done through prayer?

Prayers of intention,
Intending and praying,
Asking, receiving,
What we need today.

Is to go walking and praying,
Praying and walking,
Walking and talking,
Talking to God.

Adoration/Frustration

Stretching out
into eternity
in this hour
Peace can come
and quietness outside

Internally, though, all is busy
Thoughts speed and bounce
Hydrons colliding
Exploding upon impact
Their energy consume minutes

But there, in the gaps
Between thought explosions
Is space, sacred
Only glimpsed
Barely registering

Minutes move by
Sitting in the gaze of love
Equilibrium settles
Noise inside subsides
Space opens up

Deeper – to the core
Through layers of 'me'
Worry, joy, possessions, trivia
The journey begins
Under watchful gaze

'Come and see'
Can I get beyond 'me'?
Distracted now, frustrated
I miss the point
Minutes go by

Gentle glimpses
Of sacred space
Return as I let go
Of the need to let go
And surrender to being

Stillness, peace, love
Are within my grasp
Until I grasp
For it is' me' grasping
Grasping for what can be 'mine'

And minutes tick by
The hour almost done
The lesson of holding on learned
The invitation to let go – accepted
All the while gazed upon and loved

Surfing Life's Waves

O, to stand in the Heavenly Cove
On a grey and stormy day
Air heavy and damp
Awaiting the flow
Clouds descending

O, to wade out into the sea
Sting of cold
Shortness of breath
Heart beating
Keeping me alive

O, to feel the surge of current
Pulling this way and that
Not of me anymore
Thy will be done
God in the ocean

O, to catch a descent wave
To ride it onto shore
Muscles tense
Body tired
Connected to land once more

O, to live in a heavenly cove
Of storms and clouds
And seas and currents
Of being alive
Surfing life's waves

Eternal Mystery, Eternal Invitation

Each new day
I go to the foot of the cross
The opening of my eyes
Brings me there
And I sit
A silent witness
Of events long gone
Yet repeated evermore
Eternal mystery
Eternal invitation
To see

Some days the suffering and the pain
I feel it in my bones or heart
Wounded with the One
Or the sorrow and grief
Of a mother given
And a loyal friend, receiving her
For us
On down days it is the emptiness
Of death entombed
My self the rock, hewn
Often I see the fear across the faces
Of His followers
And see myself in their eyes
And then the women
Always the women
Standing in courageous commitment
Completing the course
Staying fast with the one they love

I sit at the foot of the cross
Undone entirely
By the total, self-sacrificing love
Of a Brother, Father, Spirit God
Pain, grief, emptiness, fear
Never the end
The promise of three days later
My own story written at the foot of the cross

This Old Cross

This old cross has been with me now
For long and many a year
I put it on religiously
And daily bend its ear

I tell this cross my innermost
I tell it all my woes
And when I do this enough
I find my worry goes

This cross lies upon my chest
Each and every day
I often reach out and touch it
To keep my troubles at bay

So, I put on this old cross
My uniform so to speak
And try to live as Jesus would
Loving, turning the other cheek

You see this cross reminds me
Of God and heaven above
Of sacrifice and holocaust
And how much we are loved

I'll wear this cross all my days
Through happiness and loss
And when I die I pray that I
Will be buried wearing my old cross

Between the Beads

There is a space between each Rosary bead
I rarely notice it at all
Hands and eyes drawn to the wood or glass itself
Yet it is there – the space
Between last word spoken and first word coming
Lies a space
How brilliant!
A space, inviting us
To?
Perhaps reflect
Perhaps rest
Perhaps act
But invite us it does
Anew each time we lift the beads
We lift the space too
Divine emptiness
To be filled with God's will
God's energy, advocate
God's love
But only if we notice
The space
We need, it seems
Some silence
Some chaos, uncontrolled
And unscripted
In order to fulfil the script

ERECTED
BY HIS FAMILY
AND
THE CONGREGATION
OF KILMUIR

Chapter 2: Death and Loss

*'Our friend Lazarus has fallen asleep; but I am
going there to wake him up.' John 11: 11*

From the time I was a little boy I have had a routine of
visiting the graves of my deceased relatives. This came
from my grandfather, Jimmy Webb, who took me most
Sundays to visit my grandmother's (his wife's) grave. Before
I had been born, Jimmy had for a long time been visiting
that grave. You see, his wife died in 1950, three short years
after they had married. She was called Agnes and she was
only 25. She died from an illness that today is treatable.
Tragic. And when Agnes passed away, she left Jimmy with
two young daughters, my aunt Christine (1 year old) and
my mother, Ann (3 years old). Jimmy never married again.
Agnes was to be his only love. And as a faithful husband
would do, Jimmy visited Agnes' grave often. As years
became decades, the visit to her grave became a focal
point of his week. And I also became part of this routine.
He would come to my house, collect me, and we would
set off. I have so many happy memories of my grandad.
We went all over the place together and we visited all
sorts of people – his friends and our family. But I have to
say that the visit to my granny's grave was a special thing
for me. I think I knew the sacredness of the moments that
we stood at her grave. We would always say a prayer. He
would always reminisce in some way. And we would talk
about what was going on in our lives. I realise now that his
visiting the grave was a way for him to keep Agnes part of

his life; part of his daily or weekly routine. It was a way for him to keep the spirit of their marriage alive.

Part of the legacy of this time in my life is that it made 'visiting' my dead relatives feel very normal and very soothing as I talked with my deceased loved ones in prayer and in my general conversation. My understanding of the existence of an afterlife assured me that as I spoke, they heard. I carried on visiting my granny's grave with my grandad right up until his death 15 years ago. Now I also visit him as he lies at last beside his young bride. This section will take us on a journey through death and loss into the hope of new and eternal life.

Read these poems and seek out God's gentleness and compassion in the midst of grief.

I See (But Only for a Moment)

I walk silently among the dead
And each one sings beautifully
In a voice so pure that
They could not possess it while living

'Our stones tell but one part of our story'
'A small and short stage while we were with you'
'And though the pain of going seems the end'
'Now we see. Now we see!'

And they sing this refrain, 'Now we see!'
In harmonies no mortal could achieve
For they are free to see, to be, to see
The oneness of all humanity

This choir soars high as I walk
Among their ranks daily
But rarely do I let myself hear it
Caught too much in my own small and short stage

But every now and then in a silent moment
And when I'm open to belief
A heavenly note rings out in life
And for a moment I see. I see!

Dying to Live

I die many times each day
Up close and personal
With my self

In small humilities
And moments of distance
Shedding the unneeded, unwanted

Travelling downward all the more
Holding onto the letting go
The lessons of death

Waiting to bottom out
And break through
Reformed, re-formed

As what has always been
Covered up falsely no more
Dying to live

The Shell of Sorrow

Inside the hard, spiky shell of sorrow
With its barbs
That wound
Is a whirlpool of all the memories we hold
Of each other
Lives entwined and lived together
The sharing of joy and laughter
The trials we overcame
The tears we shed in grief and loss

And now the loss is you
The grief we feel
For you

The pool of memories
Beyond our ability to comprehend
The turn of events
That have led us to consider them precious
Or consider them memories at all
But memories they are
Coated in the shell of sorrow
The barbs spiking us
Wounding us
Piercing us
Drawing us
To despair

Help us
From beyond our reality
This flimsy, technicolour veneer
Half story
Help us
These days to come
You, at peace now
Reunited now
Complete now
We, still holding to the shell of our sorrow
Barbed and wounded
Grieving you
Loving you

Find

Find me at the close of time
When dusk has come and gone for you too
When darkness looks like it envelopes all
I will light your path

Find me at the moment of your letting go
Of all that weighs you down –
The stone encasing your heart –
I will chip away your doubt

Find me when you let yourself be lost
Utterly at sea
Seemingly rudderless
I will guide you home

Find me in the midst of pain
When hurt consumes
And tortures the soul
I will console you

Find me though you don't believe
When you don't think that you can
Fear not
I will find you

Words for a Dead Friend

Those who have died,
And gone before us,
Witness to eternal truth.
Faith has led them there.

Death,

Only a mode of transport,
A door to be entered through;
The Way.
And our way is one of sadness,
At their going.
Of memories that pull at us.

Grief.

But more than that,
Ours is a way of hope and of faith too,
That we will meet again,
Finally,
Really,
Tender embrace awaiting us.
Smiling eyes,
Greeting us with,
'I told you so'

Past Tense Presence

When the present
Presence
Becomes the past
Tense
Sad
Tearful
Immediate experience

Space, the missing
Suddenly not 'now'
But 'memory'
When so recently
The missing
Wasn't missed
But held, heard, seen

Sensorial actuality
The painful reality
Temporal and temporary
For a short time
Feeding
The soul
Memories to come

Silence, endured
Provides the canvas
Heart, felt, the colour
Mind, open, the image
Not present – no
But deeper now and real
Past tense, presence

The Departed

The hour has come
And memories fly
So many now
Departed

Left
Leaving us
Grieving them
Missing them
Sensing them

Never more than tonight
And each night
Sting of loss
Pain of loneliness
Melancholy for the missing

Earthly senses
Keep us
Drawn to their demise
But they?
They have begun the eternal journey

Departed at last
Holding us all the while
Destination tantalising

Rising
Rising
Rising

Wounded and Wonderful

At sunset we hold,
What feels for all the world,
Like grief – spiky, painful,
Like disaster – a curtain torn in two.

Destroyed.

We hold it close despite ourselves,
In spite of ourselves and our wound,
We do all that can be done –
We lay it in the tomb of night,
And we sleep, fistful.

In REM Communion.

Dreaming dreams,
Visioning, daring to hope,
This rag tag mess,
Of grief and worry,
Devastation and the screwed up,

Somehow,

Through effusion,
Of divine wonder,
And explosive light,
Of Spirit,
Transforms,

All.

No longer jagged, craggy rock of grief,
And holocaust,
We once held despite, in spite,
We hold in joy,
The curtain mended.

One.

Seamless.
Wounded but wonderful.

Reclaimed

The dead, reclaimed
And taken back
Once more to the earth
From which they were born
Grew on, lived on
Loved on, died on
Buried there by lovers and loved ones
Forlorn, grieving, torn apart
Their resting places adorned
By stones and crosses
Bearing them proudly
For all passers-by to see

But loved ones live and die themselves
And for so many
Names once clear and memories held
Grow encased and covered up
The tomb within a tomb
Of ivy, flower and tree
Graves reclaimed, as their soul
Which flew unto Creator waiting

Birds nest, foxes hunt
Life continuing in the midst of the dead
And wayfarers on a solemn pilgrimage
To their people's resting place
Rest themselves on graves reclaimed
Finding solace on another's territory
Not knowing who lies underneath them
Nor that anyone lies there at all

All ground is hallowed
For those who see
Those who once walked on it
Were like you and me
Simply travelling through
Waiting to be reclaimed
And to be put under the earth
As souls fly unto Creator waiting

Citadel of Non-Resident Souls

To walk in the citadel of non-resident souls
Empty now
Souls gone on
Each avenue and crescent
Echoes
The stories of countless lives
Countless connections
Told in granite, marble and iron
Each word and deed
A stepping stone on the road
To this place

And at each resting place
Hooded guards stand
Winged, warriors
Watching, waiting
Mirror black
Silently staring
Calling to each other
And the dead
Only visitors here
Non-resident souls soar high above

To walk in the citadel of non-resident souls
Seemingly full of life
A reluctant, prospective occupant
Surveying the land
Content to delay purchase
For a while yet
But knowing that when the time comes
My story too will be written

In granite, marble and iron
Empty plot
Full only of ashes and dust
Non-resident soul
Flying unto the arms
Of Love

And Then the Light Got in

Lost
Frightened
Alone
And then the light got in

Blind
Deaf
Speechless
And then the light got in

Angry
Fighting
Shouting
And then the light got in

Me
Me
Me
And then the light got in

Them
Them
Them
And then the light got in

Us
We
Together
I think the light got in

Chapter 3: Relationships

'After this the Lord appointed seventy-two others and sent them two by two ahead of him to every town and place where he was about to go.'

Luke 10: 1

None of us are called to journey alone. We are called to walk the path of life together and to be in communion with each other. We find this communion with family, friends, neighbours work colleagues and those we encounter in daily life. We need each other – more than we know most of the time. That's not to say that it is easy to share our life journey with others. Sometimes it is very difficult to stand in true relationship with each other. And yet, when we do, we are really acting out of God's plan for us. There is something wonderful at the core of all people and when we spend time looking for it in ourselves and each other we find it and we can revel in it.

This chapter will offer poems and prayer moments for us all as we try to be in communion with God, ourselves and each other.

A Father's Eyes

In a father's eyes shine bright
The memories of the child's growth
From birth to babe to beginning
To spread their wings

Behind a father's eyes loom large
The moments of joy and sorrow
The moments of pride and regret
As life's journey winds on

Through a father's eyes it's clear
What a gift to the world all children are
The unbounded possibilities of their lives
Waiting to be fulfilled – watch out world!

In front of a father's eyes
The babies are no more
Dependence becomes inter-dependence
The caring goes both ways

For a father's eyes begin
To grow old and weak
And yet when they are closed in memory
The laughter of the children brings tears of joy

Not so Random Act of Kindness

Sometimes an ordinary grey day
All rain teaming down and traffic jams
Can be ripped gloriously apart
By an act of kindness

Kindness so staggeringly selfless
Like true kindness always is
That it brings technicolour joy
And time, momentarily, stands still

In that moment of kindness received
One is humbled by the act – who am I to receive it?
In awe of the kindness that IS the person giving
And visited by God's gentle touch

Grey days, all rain and traffic jams
Ripped gloriously apart
By God's breath
Breathed out in kindness

Me

This old face
Is what the world sees
Once taut skin
Taught by experience
To loosen up
Stretches, wrinkled and creased
Across flesh and bone
Creating a visual, visage
Recognised by friends
Loved by family
But curious to the one
Looking out from it
These eyes see
Others' faces more often
And catch only glimpses
Of their own
And ask
Who is that?
Is that me?
Fresh faced boy
Watches internally
Fascinated by the wrapper
Covering his youth

Greying hairs
Heavy beard
Marks of life lived
Well
Well, in the main
In the mane
White sparkles
Enveloping the brown
Colonising the crown
Confirming the march
Onwards, ageing
This old face
Wrinkled and creased
Baggy-eyed and tired
Can laugh, cry, smile, frown
Can carry messages of love
Hate too – on a bad day
Searches out other faces
To recognise and be with
To watch as they grow old
In sympathy perhaps
This old face – is me.

Could Have...

All the things I could have done
Would have done
Should have done
If all the things I should have done
Were possible to do

All the things I nearly said
I wished I'd said
Or hadn't said
If all the words I could have said
Were said from me to you

All the love I never shared
I would have shared
Gladly shared
If all the love I never shared
I'd shared firstly with me

All the hugs I longed to give
I ached to give
Freely to give
If all the hugs I longed to give
Were given, then truly hugged you'd be

Alphabetical Order

Align yourself to all that is love, joy and mercy

Believe that this is not only possible but necessary to truly be alive

Concede in humility that there is much more we don't know than we do know

Demonstrate this by being curious about others and their standpoint

Explore this world and this life by reading, talking, watching and praying

Find the goodness within you and sit with that, ignoring all that draws you from this goodness

God is goodness. God is love, joy and mercy. God is so much more than we can describe. God is waiting for us. Now!

Have a great day, every day. On the not so great days, remember that you will have better days

Imagine a better world and then do something about it

Join something – a club, a church, a political party, a cause. We're better together than alone

Kiss someone today. Cheek or lips, decide between you!

Love. That is all

Make someone's day through a completely random act of kindness. It'll make your day too

Never give up on yourself. You are not finished yet

Open a new book today. Read and wonder.

Play more often. We are told that playing games is childish.
And that is correct. But being childish is class!!

Quality, not quantity, is what counts when it comes to most
things in life – prayers, friends, and talents to name but a few

Remember that God exists and that God loves you

Stop right now. Stop whatever you are doing. Take a minute to
pray for someone who needs a prayer right now

Thankfulness is a great quality to have and a skill that can be
practiced. Practice it often

Understand others' points of view as being the best that they
can do in this moment. Take the conversation on from that
position and see how it develops

Volunteer some of your time, money or resources to an organi-
sation that does good in the world

Words can hurt just as much as slaps or punches. Use them
wisely and for love

Xenophobia makes no sense whatsoever. If you were in another country, you'd be afraid of yourself!

You are special. Go you!!

Zest for life will probably lengthen the life we live or, at least,
make it seem zingier!

In the Gym for the Soul

Daily workouts
Daily working out
Working it out
In the gym for the soul
What's it all about?
Deep in my soul
What is all about?
In the world in which my soul exists
Weighty topics
To be lifted
Pumped
And contemplated
In the gym for the soul
What will we find?
If we go deep into the soul
Who will be waiting for us there?
It will be the Meaning
The Beginning and the End all in one
Knowable
In the gym for the soul
Sweating it out
Sweating out confusion
Profusion of doubt
Drinking in wonder and awe
Strengthening the muscles
Of the mind and soul
Starting to see
Definition
Trimming and cutting

The dark and the reasonless
Building the light and the purpose
Connection of thought and emotion
To Spirit and Wisdom
Becoming what my soul already is
A journey alone
Is twice the distance
Soul mates along the way
Keep the motivation high
Encourage moments of learning
And insight
To myself
Encourage regular returns
To the gym for the soul

Chapter 4: Facing Hardships

'In my distress I called to Yahweh and to my God I cried; from his temple he heard my voice, my cry came to his ears.' Psalm 18: 6

It is the nature of all of our lives that there come times when we face into hardship. This hardship can take many forms, of course. For some it will be illness or even impending death. For others it will come in the form of relationship difficulties or break ups. Still others will face poverty, injury, exclusion, poor self-esteem, addiction, or bereavement. We can look around and see so many people coping with so much. In fact we are often blown away and amazed by just how much some people have to cope with in their lives and just how well they carry their burden. This chapter is dedicated to the people in our lives who are facing hardships – and this might be you at this time. The poems that follow draw attention to the hardships that people face and encourage us all to remember those who suffer in our prayers and to reach out in love to them in our actions. It has been said that prayer which does not end in action, is not prayer at all.

The Bag Man

I was born some time ago
With tiny bags grafted onto each hair follicle
Tiny, invisible collecting bags
They floated emptily
From my new-born hair
Happy, little kites helping me to float
Helplessly, easily
Into life

But collecting bags collect
Things, people, memories, dreams
Wishes, regrets, real or not
All collected in the bags

It is a curious fact
That the nature of the collecting bag
Is such
That the difficult things weigh a little more
Than the happy things
Go figure, but it seems to be
And so....

Nowadays the bags can get heavy
And on some days
Rather than lift me, floating
They make each step
A drag
Legs a little heavier

Mind a little slower
Day a little darker
The bags, you see
Real or not, get full up
And I slow down

But oh, the joy!
On a day when the scissors
Cut loose a bag or two
It does happen
Through forgiveness, reconciliation, closure
Bag gone
Through sifting the real from the imaginary
Bag gone
Through contact, connection and cuddles
Bag gone

And the freedom
No words
Just lightness
Just stillness
Just a beautiful sense
Of being... ok
I am the bag man

Eaten

Loneliness, a disease
That eats at the core
Of a being
Being

Sometimes alone
Surrounded by distant
Strangers, known
Unknown

The drip, drip
Of emptiness deafening
The person within
Outside

Unbreakable barriers
Real and imagined
Keep its prisoner
Imprisoned

Nothing, huge
The path a battle
The walker weary
Weary

Church of the Emergency Department

There's a blood stained tissue on the waiting room floor
And a young girl crying just outside the door
Broken bones, broken hearts and a whole lot more
In the Church of the Emergency Department

The congregation gathers for nightly prayer
Each one of them wishing that they weren't there
The victims, their families, the staff that care
All in the Church of the Emergency Department

The drinking and fighting and accidents routine
The sick and the dying all wait to be seen
Some healed, some not, some somewhere between
Welcome to the Church of the Emergency Department

Spare a thought out here if you're feeling well
For the ones who gather with stories to tell
Of illness or sadness or a living hell
Tales of the Church of the Emergency Department

A Boat for a Heart All at Sea

When the waves come
As they will, as they must
And you find your heart
Tossed and turned, all at sea
Arms flailing
All worry and panic

Stop

Rest for a while
Allow the waves
To take you where they will

Be

Calm your beating heart
Your constant doing
Breathe

Feel still

And in the stillness
Clarity will come, dawning

Realisation

And with it, a boat
Carried by boisterous waves
Though gliding as if carefree
A top the stormy seas

Coming
For you

Waiting
For you
To climb in
And, once aboard
Your heart, too
Will glide, as if carefree
While all around the waves,
As they will, as they must
Roll and crash with
Foam and fury

Friends now

Not destroying, but
Energising
Bringing boats for
Hearts all at sea

Dark Days, Gone

Dark days, blue days
Days that grind, and slow
Different eyes, tired eyes
Eyes that cease to glow

Up's down, down's up
Up, down, down once more
Round and round, dizzy now
Heart falls to the floor

Words come, words go
Words, to talk is sore
So emptiness rules, silence cuts
Cuts me to the core

Dark days brighten up
Bright sunshine come alive
Landscapes open up
Let me walk in them and thrive

Dark days, blue days
Grind yourselves away
Be gone, now be gone
Please, be gone and gone to stay

Freedom of Days

My wish for you

On this day and all,

Is simply this;

That you would have

The freedom of days.

Free days,

With free breathing

In an easy chest.

And free feeling

In a light heart.

Free movement

In confident steps,

Towards the free embrace

Of a lover's arms.

I pray you find this freedom.

It's yours,

Not needing to be won

Or deserved

At all

It's yours, yours;

Gratuitous gifting,

Good

Gracefully given.

Find the freedom.

Claim it

In slow breaths

And comfortable chairs,

With deep, heart-music

And stroke of loved one's hand

On shoulder or brow.

Discover it in silence,

In self-gift of stopping, listening;

Retuning perspective and priorities.

Find my wish for you

Already there and waiting.

Homeless in Manhattan

'I have bad days'
He looks at me and says quietly
Clutching himself
Under a frayed army issue jacket
His cardboard sign
Lies on the sidewalk
'Homeless and hungry. Please help'
Accidental alliteration
Announcing the adversity
This man faces
In a city with too much
We throw away more than we need
Too much
But not for all
'I have bad days'
He manages a smile now
As he pets his dog (skinny, loving him back)
'But I believe God has a plan
For better things to come'
He looks at me longingly
For some reflected confirmation
That God exists
And his plan is not for all bad days
'I believe it is so', I nod
We sit in silence now
Connected
Both petting a dog

Both sitting on a sidewalk
In this city of excess
Both begging God
For an end to bad days

Little Prayers Answered

Little prayers answered
Can easily go by
Without us recognising
The real reason why
This worked out
Or that wee worry
Simply passed us by
And that special person
Got the one thing
That they needed more than desired
But if we stopped
And counted our blessings
We'd see miracles we can't deny
And we'd give our thanks
Where they belong
To Our Father
Our eternal ally

For Anyone Crying Today

Tears
Are funny things
When funny things happen
Magnifying the humour
Magic in the moment

Tears
Blind us
A safety wall
Between us
And terrible realities

Tears
Cleanse us
A good cry
Brings forth
The untold and un-tellable

Tears
Bond us
To intimate space friends
When shed and shared
In precious moments of union

Tears
Remind us
Bringing a physical reality
The presence of those lost
Shouting of the existence of love

Tears
Flow, stream down faces
Rivers of emotion, natural and of God
Our inner strength in watery form
Don't dry your eyes

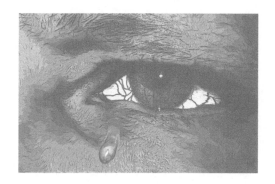

Chapter 5: Mountain Moments

'Very early in the morning, while it was still dark, Jesus got up, left the house and went off to a solitary place, where he prayed.' Mark 1: 35

I live in Belfast, Northern Ireland. Belfast is essentially a bowl surrounded by hills and mountains. The part of the city that I live in affords me easy access to part of this network of hills and mountains. Thank God at this time in my life I still have the ability to spend good stretches of time walking. I do so every day at some point. It is often while out in the world around me that I feel most connected to God and most connected to the spiritual life. Whether it is in meeting horses in the Hatchet Field high above West Belfast or seeing the beauty of butterflies floating by on Divis Mountain or indeed just hearing the voice of God on the wind, there is something in taking myself out of the comfort of my own home that feels good.

In this chapter, I invite you to share some of these mountain moments with me.

Trinity of the Day

Morning

Sun rises over a city mountain.
Our petrified friend
Kept watch o'er us
As sleep took us
And dreams and visions
Filled the emptiness.
The mountain, faithful
Ever present,
Hands the day over
To the sun
And all is new.
All light once again
Trinity of the Day

Midday

Mid-day over the lough.
A moment to stand still.
Bathing
In what has been so far
Today.
Time in the present;
A moment to examine
What happened around us,
Seeing it for what it was.
Giving thanks
For the scent of Good Spirit
Guiding, leading, pruning.
Acknowledging
Stray steps
Away from the path.
Mid-day moment
Allowing for a beginning
Amidst what had already begun;
Days within days.

Night

Sun sets over the lough
In blood orange reds
That peel back the layers of the day,
Drawing us to pause in wonder;
Widening eyes and consciousness.
Imprinting fire and shadows
On retina, optic nerve and brain.
Sun sets,
On me,
On you,
On all that has gone before;
Disappointments as much as joys,
Exploding, imploding, eroding
Uploading the impending night.
Pure darkness
To be torn asunder once more
At dawn
As
Sun rises over the lough.

The Ancient Paths

I stood where there are no new paths
And found the ancient ones
Feeling them more than seeing
I followed them upwards
To the mountain

Climbing, digging feet and nails into muck
I went up, sometimes down
Not looking too far ahead
For fear of losing heart and chance
To meet the one who awaited me

Exhausted, my breath as clouds enveloped me
I fell to the floor in silent prayer
Would I never rise to the place where I can see?
Was I to be a blind pilgrim, alone?
Onwards, I pulled myself up and found the ancient path again

Fear, anxiety, scorn and shame
Rushed at me from every dark shadow
And clawed at my feet from the very ground below
One step begged another to join it
Muscle, tendon, cartilage and sinew screamed

Then an oddity of sorts
A small wild flower appeared alone
Fragile, yet vital, it smiled at me
Vivid yellow and green it blinded
The dark and shadows paled, vanquished

Renewed energy, pulsing optimism
Clarity of vision and purpose grew
One step was joined by another
The ancient paths called 'hosanna'
Their revered one awaited me above – onwards!

Definitive, Rock

The vast green plain
Burning peat in the morning sun
Opens up
The line of sight

Far off mountain tops
Crisp and clear
Almost touchable
Definitive, rock

Step along the path
Strangers met
With smiling eyes
Drinking in the same sights

No suspicion, no distance
Fellow travellers
Well met
We pass by

And on the feet go
Taking us deeper
Into field and gorse
Cow and horse

Observe us
Sweaty, moving on a hot day
Foolish to them
As they seek shadow and lie

No rest for us
A path to be walked
Drunk now on nature
More, more, more!

Sea of white
Wings lighter than air
Butterflies flutter by
Urging us to follow

Larks sing
A hymn to this place
Notes soaring with them
And my soul too.

Feet on earth
Eyes on the world
Heart
On Divis

Fallen

I fell today
On a high mountain path
I stumbled on old familiar rocks
Rising up at me again

And so I fell
The going down as if in slow motion
The shame that others might see my fall
Replaced by the beauty of the scenery going by

I tumbled around
Until I didn't know if I was going down or up
The world inverted with me in it
Fallen, astounded by beauty

As I lay there
Presumably at rock bottom
A butterfly flitted about me
'Avila!', I cried from my soul's depth

I reached out
To hold the butterfly just beyond my worldly grasp
But in the reaching towards her
I had unknowingly stood again

Upright, for now
I walked on in thanksgiving
For the descent
And the beauty of getting back up

Summer Rain

The smell of summer rain
Dry earth soaking
Life bursting through
Green emerging from the blue
Clearness of the water

On the river bank
Life's moments floating by
Let go
And drifting away
To their rightful destination

Sitting on soil
Holding me in time and place
Grounding me
To the energy of all things
Flowing, pulsing, God's love

My Beloved Divis

Alive, wise and proud
Looking over the city below
A grandparent seeing
The youngster growing up
Every half century
This city consumes itself
In bullets, flames and stones
Divis looks on
Lovingly
At a city so close
To what it can be
And addicted to
False victories

Every year its people more closer
To the Divis foothills
Subconsciously drawn to
Its solace
With them they bring
The vandals' fire
And the politicos'
Bed linen staked
Messages of hate
And hurt
Still, Divis stands
Evidence of the eternal movement
Death to resurrection
Its green fields grow silently
Through charred earth
Christ in the mountain

Perhaps one day all will live
On the mountain
The city, emptied
Given a chance to grow, quiet
Breath of relief
My road and your road
Will become… roads
Birds will nest there
And over time, cows and sheep
Will descend with caution

From farmland
To the empty streets
People will look down then
And tell their great-grandchildren
'Humans lived there once.
But not fully.'
The mountain will keep them safe
Fires will burn for heat only
Stones will move for shelter
Far below, the city's dividing walls
Will crumble
Grass will grow thick there
The mountain and city
Will become as one

For now, I'll climb to Divis' summit
And look down
At a city so close
To what it can be
And addicted to

False victories
Thanking God for his mountain
For the story of resurrection it retells
And try to take this story
Back down with me

A Belfast River

I caught the smell of a Belfast river today

As I walked past

In a wet and windy wander, wondering

The smell

Not altogether pleasant

Part muck

Part rotten food

Part metal shopping trolley

Testament to the detritus

Of everyday life

Cast from the banks

Into the flow

The smell

Caught me unawares

Caused me to stop

I was a young boy again

Playing with sticks in this river

The weather was better

As it always is in memories

The heat from the sun

Warming the water

Intensifying the smell

So it filled my young nostrils

Till all was this river, the smell and the sticks

The smell

Stronger then

The river teaming

Full of the things we didn't want to keep

We were not so environmentally green then

But we spent more time in the environment

Thumbs sore from catching hurling balls

Not from X-Box fatigue

The smell

I was a young man now

I walked along this river's banks

The smell my companion

As I tried to find meaning

In the killing and dying

Of my youth

The river flowed by me then

Into a divided city

Barricades and bombs

Bullets and blood

Thirsty speeches of hate

The river saw it all

And so did I

The smell

I was a young father and husband

In times of fledgling cessation

And tentative talking

Hands nearly shook

That had never contemplated

Such an act

My children grew

Playing by this river

Smelling this very smell

The smell

It will remind my children of laughter

I hope

Their laughter

Flowing now through our city

Freely moving

Like the wise, old, smelly river

The smell

Still the smell

Still the river

Still the city

Still us

Chapter 6: New Life and Love

'I have come that they may have life, and have it to the full.' John 10: 10

What a wonderful thing it would be to be a true presence of love in the world. We can all call to mind someone or some people we have met along the way who were just that. We can see how they enriched the world and those they met by giving, loving, praying, advising and comforting. These people are truly a gift to the world. We often say that 'God is love'. To truly love is to be truly God-orientated.

This section celebrates the best in life and love and encourages us to bring new life to the world around us by reaching out in love to those we meet along the way.

Peace Rain

May peace rain down on us,

Like huge drops of cold water,

Falling in the desert,

Of life's experience,

Where there is war,

And fear and confusion.

Fall upon us.

Soak into and through us.

Take away the dry,

And the barren,

Perversions of violence,

And torture and apathy.

Shock us,

Cold rain of peace,

Into action,

Inertia conversion,

Energy, outwards,

Generous and saving.

Wash away the horror,

Longed for rain of peace.

Wash clean the misdeeds.

Wash anew the heavy hearts,

Of the downtrodden,

Me's and you's.

Rain down right now,

In this moment and all,

Like tongues of spirit fire,

Opening hearts,

Flooding minds,

Uniting people.

May we dance for rain,

In our praying,

And in our campaigning.

And may the clouds respond.

Deluge, drowning all in its path,

Leaving only peace.

Bloom, Eternally

New life blooms,

Where once we thought was only death.

What felt like an end, was,

In fact,

A transition.

Indeed,

It was a necessary precursor,

To a blooming hitherto unfathomable.

A growth into fully being.

Our being here,

Though wonderful,

Is, it would appear,

Only a warming up,

For the main event.

And One who died,

Did so,

And so,

We who live now,

Will live eternal.

Flowers, grass and tree,

In a heavenly garden,

Blown by Divine breezes,

Surrounded by those we love.

For a Lover

If I were a poet,
The words I would write,
Would capture for all time,
Your eyes
As they well up,
With silver transparent tear diamonds;
Freezing a moment,
As you begin to laugh.

And the words I would write,
Would tell of the flips,
The butterflies in my belly perform,
As they anticipate your breathless laugh.

And the extra beat,
My heart booms,
At your joyous giggle explosion;
Infectious to all in its blast radius.

My words would capture,
The purest expression of happiness,
Your body emits,
In shoulder shudder and chuckle.

And the absolute,
Light-being,
You are.

Alas, I am no poet.
And my words fall sadly short.

I can but revel,
Indulgently in your moment,
Of humour –
Consumed by you,
And utterly in love.

It's Only Natural

Then the sun shone bright
And I suddenly knew
That no matter what
This life threw
At me, at us
At them, at you
We'd do alright
And we'd get through

The wind blew cool
And kissed my brow
And drew me to
The here and now
And broke me from
My pow wow wow
Of poor me past
And peace did allow

The trees grew tall
And shouted to me
'Like us you are
Called and permitted to be
What you really are
Not just what others see'
Wisdom in nature
The sun, wind and tree

Heart, Beat

In a heartbeat
All is changed
There is nothing to fear
Here is all, full – we exhale at last

The sound of a heartbeat
Not so much a sound as an ultra-sound
Smashing and crashing and booming
Into life and life into the heart

The heart that beats is strong
Joy! With a journey yet to come
But we know, we believe
The beat goes on – heart, beat

Bloom

Burst out
In glorious you-colour
Spreading outwards
Upwards towards the sun

Light reflected
Your technicolour
For all to witness
Blinded by joy

Obscenely bright
Over the top
Multi coloured
You – great!

By osmosis
The world will drink you in
And give back out
Your essential core

Others will sprout
Shoots of hope
Petals of love
Blooming marvellous you

Burn and Blow

Give me a tongue of fire
To warm me from within
To rekindle the love in me
Of me, for me, from me

The flame dwindled
Rekindled in furious passion
For things, all things
And all be-ings

Give me a breath of wind
Fresh air for the soul
Cobwebs blasted away
Sails, set and full

Galeforce love and will to show
Love, forgiveness and compassion
Blow me onwards
Outwards, inwards, you-wards

Give me heat and air
Oxygen for the flames
Fill me up with them
and let me loose

Poem for a Book

I bought a book today
Almost by chance
It called to me as I walked by
Butterfly cover – soft in colour
Lightness appealing
Hidden, empty pages
Yearning to be filled
Accepting of ramblings
Searching for beautiful words
To describe ordinary things
Ugly things as well
Will be captured
Like butterflies in a net
To be kept, admired
Remembered, looked upon.

Today, I'll open the butterfly book
Step into it and find
What's in its void
Fear of emptiness continuing
Of nothing left to say
Flies in the face of everything
Yet to be discovered
Recovered, re-discovered

Opened up anew
Butterfly book
Give me ears to hear
And eyes to see!
That which already swirls
And pulses through the universe

The infinite possibility of being
The in-dwelling of Spirit
In all, already and always.

And seen, heard
I commit to you
Butterfly book
The ramblings of my Spirit
The private place made public
Rebirth through pen and paper.

It Begins

This day, begun
Is a thousand years to come
Ten thousand lie ahead
We stand at the doorway today
Of love, joy and mercy

The night, ended
Brought to a close
Millions of years
Finished, finally
And with them, hurt, fear and death

Night, ended
Day, begun
Wonderful divide
Re-consecration
And we are here!

Awesome Day

There is no ordinary
There is no normal
There is no routine

There is newness each day
There is a fingerprint uniqueness
There is the sky

There is a rhythm
There is a beat
There is a place for you in the band

There is grounding
There is flight
There is movement all around

There is heat
There is light
There is energy

There is me
There is you
There is God

Filing

Silver sunset in a city park
Light fades on another day
Its events now filed under 'past'
Gone? Only brought to life
By memories
Wistful, nostalgic, thankful or hurt
Their power in reality
Dissipated
The moment they ceased to be
Felt alive nonetheless
Their energy, synapse impulsivity
Day ending
Night coming
And with it morning
Screaming into birth
With golden sun
In a city park rising
Light illuminating
New experiences
Hearts beat, beings meet
So much more life
More possibility
So much undecided yet
File empty
Beautifully so
Yearning to be filled well
Live only in it

Cold Nights Busking on Belfast City Streets

String tracks cut into fingertips
The indentations of every note ever he's played
The grooves in his fingers more numerous
    than the coins in his pocket
Playing finished, fingers rest
Blood begins to flow again
And with the blood, pain
Shoppers rush by
Ears tickled by piped muzak
Emanating from the new temples
Of materialistic fundamentalism
Barely noticing the lone guitarist
Counting the coins
Counting the cost
Driven to search for the tone
The notes
The one line so full
That it says it all
Rest over, the search continues
Fingers play, voice swells
Pain alleviated
Bright colours of magical tunes
Envelope him, invisible to all
But the discerning few
The caring few
The few who know
Music
Music is life

O New Day

Leap into life
Experience the breath as if a first
Rise of the chest
Signalling intake
Fall again
As we ready ourselves
To breathe again
Precious, unconscious routine
Stuff of life itself

Rejoice in each face
As if a long lost love
Rediscovered jewel
Reflection of the maker himself
Savour that face
Bask in its beauty
Linger, long, loving it
Give thanks for the company
Intimacy, knowing

Greet each problem
As an opportunity
Solution in acceptance
And in suffering quietly
Uniting the self with the Source
Praying for others' growth
As we diminish
Knowing that someone else
Is holding us in our need

Meet yourself anew today
Introduction to a soul
Tried and trying
Loved and loving
Failing and falling
A work in progress
And progress is made
Another step backwards
To where we began

Open your eyes
Start the day
Allow the light to get in
Banishing darkness
Flooding photo receptors
Bursting gloriously
Each glimmer, each shadow
A gift to behold
And hold, this is it

Go on

One step at a time.

Breathe after each step.

Drink in the air

And the achievement

That one step is.

Only after recognition

Of the step honestly taken

And the effort afforded it

Do you need to contemplate

The next step.

And then step.

Step gently.

Step in confidence

That you are not stepping alone.

No.

Others step too.

One at a time with you.

Look to the side

Every now and then.

See them.

Smile.

Recognise their effort.

And appreciate their steps

Even if taken differently to yours.

A step

Is

A step

After all.

In your smiling at them

See that they smile too at you.

And above all

One watches

All steps

All steppers

Loving and willing on

Each step taken

Along the road

Towards the goal

We seek.

Endless

The endless road
What a joy
No end
Imagine for one minute
No end in sight

No end at all

Only now, here, this
This square inch or so
That you occupy
On the road

No pressure to reach the end
No end, you see

Destination moot
Current position
Sum total
Of where you are
And where you'll ever be

Traveller always
Endless road of possibilities
And adventure
Ahead